W9-ASC-276

ROWING, SAILING, AND OTHER SPORTS ON WATER

by Jason Page

CONTENTS

Crabtree Publishing Company
www.crabtreebooks.com

Editor: Robert Walker

Proofreader: Mike Hodge

Acknowledgements: We would like to thank Ian Hodge, Rosalind Beckman, Ben Hubbard and Elizabeth Wiggans for their assistance.

Cartoons by: John Alston

Picture Credits: t = top, b = bottom, l = left, r = right, OFC = outside front cover, OBC = outside back cover, IFC =front cover
Ingrid Abery/ Action Plus: 12/13c. Allsport; IFC, 3br, 4t, 4/5 (main pic), 7tr, 11tr, 18/19c, 19bl, 20/21 (main pic), 25t, 26/27 (main pic), 27tr, 28/29 (main pic), 30t. Cancan Chu/ Getty Images: 14/15b. Empics; 16/17 (main pic), 17r, 22/23 (main pic), 24/25 (main pic), 28br, 30/31 (main pic). Evaristo SA/ AFP/ Getty Images: OFC. Kos Picture Source; 2/3 (main pic), 8/9 (main pic), 20/21b. Clive Mason/ Getty Images: 12b, 14/15t. PPL; 10/11 (main pic), 22t. Sipa Press/ Rex Features: 8t. Jamie Squire/ Getty Images: 20t.
Picture research by Image Select

Library and Archives Canada Cataloguing in Publication

Page, Jason
   Rowing, sailing, and other sports on the water / Jason Page.

(The Olympic sports)
Includes index.
ISBN 978-0-7787-4017-9 (bound).--ISBN 978-0-7787-4034-6 (pbk.)

   1. Boats and boating--Juvenile literature. 2. Olympics--Juvenile literature. I. Title. II. Series: Page, Jason. Olympic sports.

GV770.5.P33 2008   j797.1   C2008-900975-4

Library of Congress Cataloging-in-Publication Data

Page, Jason.
   Rowing, sailing, and other sports on the water / Jason Page.
      p. cm. -- (The Olympic sports)
   Includes index.
   ISBN-13: 978-0-7787-4017-9 (rlb)
   ISBN-10: 0-7787-4017-X (rlb)
   ISBN-13: 978-0-7787-4034-6 (pb)
   ISBN-10: 0-7787-4034-X (pb)
   1. Aquatic sports--Juvenile literature. 2. Olympics--Juvenile literature. I. Title. II. Series.

   GV770.5. P354 2008
   797--dc22
                                        2008005006

Crabtree Publishing Company

www.crabtreebooks.com   1-800-387-7650

Published in Canada
Crabtree Publishing
616 Welland Ave.
St. Catharines, Ontario
L2M 5V6

Published in the United States
Crabtree Publishing
PMB16A
350 Fifth Ave., Suite 3308
New York, NY 10118

WATER SPORTS

Grab your life jacket and prepare to set sail, as competitors take to the water in the Olympic sailing, rowing, and canoeing events!

CANCELLED!

Sailing and rowing events were supposed to have been included in the very first modern Olympics back in 1896, but the weather was so bad that the organizers had to cancel the competitions. As a result, both sports had to wait until 1900 to make their Olympic debuts.

SOMETHING OLD

People have been using boats to race on water for thousands of years. One of the earliest examples we know about dates back to 2500 BCE, when the ancient Egyptians held rowing races on the River Nile.

SUPER STATS

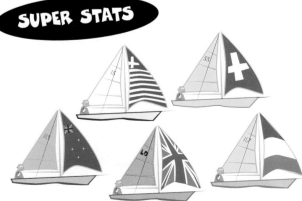

Five countries have attended every single Olympic Games since the competition began in 1896. They are: Australia, Great Britain, France, Greece and Switzerland.

SOMETHING NEW

In a way, sailing made its Olympic debut in Sydney, as it became the first Olympic sport to have a name change. The sport was previously known as "yachting." A new sailing event called the 49er was also introduced at Sydney.

Sailing in a 49er

OLYMPICS FACT FILE

⚓ The Olympic Games were first held in Olympia, in ancient Greece, around 3,000 years ago. They took place every four years until they were abolished in 393 CE.

⚓ A Frenchman called Pierre de Coubertin (1863–1937) revived the Games, and the first modern Olympics were held in Athens in 1896.

⚓ The modern Games have been held every four years since 1896, except in 1916, 1940, and 1944, due to war. Special 10th-anniversary Games took place in 1906.

⚓ The symbol of the Olympic Games is five interlocking colored rings. Together, they represent the five original continents from which athletes came to compete in the Games.

WHAT A RECORD!

The most successful competitor in any water sport was the Danish single-handed yachtsman Paul Elvström. In 1960, he became the first person in Olympic history to win four gold medals in a row in the same event. His Olympic career lasted for 40 years, and he attended eight Games from 1948 to 1988 — another record!

Paul Elvström (DAN)

The board is steered by moving the sail using this oval-shaped "boom" (or "wish-bone").

The sail is attached to a pole called the "mast," which swivels, enabling the sail to be turned in any direction.

A small fin, called a "skeg" on the underside of the board makes it more stable and helps keep it on course.

All competitors must wear life jackets.

Sailboarding

Foot straps stop the competitor's feet from slipping off the board.

DID YOU KNOW?

⅋ The RS:X is the only event in which competitors are not penalized for bumping into the buoys.

⅋ Sailboarders usually compete barefoot as this improves their grip on the board.

⅋ Sailboard competitors use the transparent window in the sail to help them see where they are going.

BUOY OH BOY!

As in other sailing events, competitors in the RS:X have to race around a course marked out using floating markers called "buoys" (pronounced "boys"). Each race takes about an hour to complete.

MAKING YOUR POINT

Like most Olympic sailing competitions, the RS:X events are decided by a series of 11 "fleet" races, so called because every competitor takes part in all the races. Competitors are awarded points according to the order in which they cross the finish line — one point for coming first, two for coming second and so on. The winner is the person with the lowest score.

RS:X

Stick a sail on a surfboard and what do you get? The answer is a sailboard — although it goes by many other names!

WHAT'S IN A NAME?

The RS:X is the event previously known as the mistral. It is also commonly known as board sailing, surfboarding, windgliding, sail boarding, and windsurfing.

Competitors need strong arms, agility, and a superb sense of balance if they want to become a sailboarding champion like Lee Lai-shan (left), of Hong Kong.

SUPER STATS

The greatest speed ever achieved on a sailboard is over 56 MPH (90.1 km/h) — that's 10 times quicker than the fastest Olympic swimmer!

Women: Faustine Merret (FRA)

SINGLE-HANDED

In the single-handed dinghy events, each boat is sailed by one person alone.

SAILING COURSE

To test the sailors' skills, the Olympic sailing courses are designed so that the wind blows in different directions in different parts of the course.

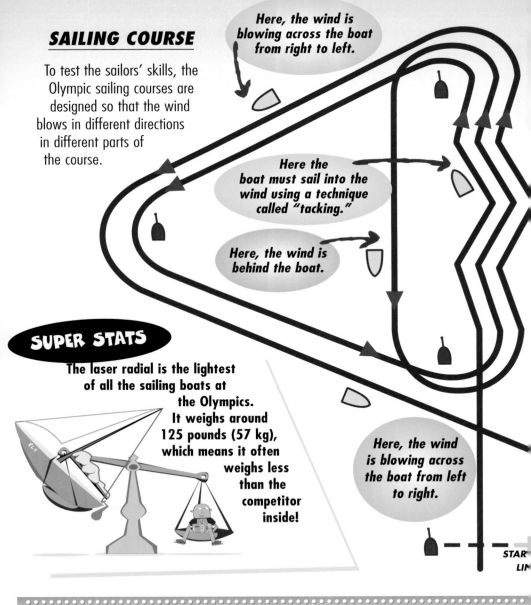

Here, the wind is blowing across the boat from right to left.

Here the boat must sail into the wind using a technique called "tacking."

Here, the wind is behind the boat.

SUPER STATS

The laser radial is the lightest of all the sailing boats at the Olympics. It weighs around 125 pounds (57 kg), which means it often weighs less than the competitor inside!

Here, the wind is blowing across the boat from left to right.

START LINE

TAKE A HIKE

A strong wind can cause a boat to capsize. To prevent this, competitors use a technique called "hiking out" — they lean out over the water, using their own body weight to balance the force of the wind and keep their boats upright. Here, Ben Ainslie (GBR), the 2004 Finn class gold medalist, shows us how it's done.

SMALLER AND SMALLER

Sailing made its Olympic debut the 1900 Olympics, and has appeared at every Olympics since 1908 — but the sailing events have changed greatly. The trend in recent years has moved toward using smaller boats with smaller crews. The early Olympic games featured boats with up to 12 crew members. At the 2008 Olympics, the largest possible crew can be made up of only three people!

TACKLING TACKING

The hardest part of the course is the stretch that sails into the wind, so here yachtsmen use a technique called "tacking." They sail forwards in a zig-zag path, but setting the sails at exactly the right angle and judging when to change course requires great skill.

WIND

FINISHING LINE

DID YOU KNOW?

Olympic events involving boats with sails was officially renamed sailing at the Sydney Olympics.

Single-handed dinghies are also called "monotypes."

At the 1988 Games, Lawrence Lemieux (CAN) was awarded a special medal for rescuing another yachtsman who was swept out to sea after capsizing.

Laser: Robert Scheidt (BRA) / Laser radial: This was a new event, so it was not held at the 2004 Games.

> This sail is called the "mainsail" or "mainsheet."

TRAPEZE ACT

On a 470, one crew member (the helmsman) steers the boat while the other hikes out. By attaching a wire (known as a trapeze) to his harness, he is able to lean right out over the water. Above, you can see Paul Foerster and Kevin Burnham (USA) the reigning men's champions in action.

DID YOU KNOW?

〽 At the Olympics, all the crew members in a boat must be of the same nationality.

〽 The 470 was invented in 1963 and immediately became one of the most popular small sailing boats.

〽 Like most other sailing events, the 49er class is decided by a series of fleet races; unlike the others, there are 16 races.

> The 49er class dinghies have a double trapeze. This means that both crew members can hike out together and set the sails to catch more of the wind, and so increase their speed.

THE 407 & 49ER

In the 470 class, men and women compete in separate events, but the 49er competition is an open event.

49er with spinnaker

DOUBLE-HANDED DINGHIES

The 49er is only two Olympics old after making its debut at the 2000 Games.

This sail, called a "spinnaker," is used for extra speed when the wind is behind the boat.

IN A SPIN

Sailors who break one of the rules of sailing must perform a penalty. This involves sailing around in a circle either once or twice, depending on the boat and the rule broken. If a penalty is not performed properly, sailors risk disqualification.

The small sail in front of the mainsail is called the "jib."

ANIMAL OLYMPIANS

With a top speed of around 42 MPH (67.6 km/h), the 49er may be the fastest boat at the Games but it's not as fast as the blue-fin tuna, which can travel over 46 MPH (74 km/h).

THE STAR

The Star is another double-handed sailing event, but unlike the double-handed dinghy competitions, the boats in this category have fixed keels.

STARTER'S SIGNAL

Six minutes before the start of each race, officials in a boat next to the starting line give a signal by firing a cannon or sounding a loud horn. One minute later, another signal is given. A third signal is given one minute before the start of the race. The fourth means the race has started.

Inspecting the keel

LEARN THE LINGO

Luff — to sail into the wind

Beat — part of the course that forces the crew to "luff"

Knot — the speed of boats is often measured in knots:
1 knot equals 1.15 MPH (1.85 km/h)

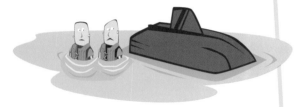

UNSINKABLE YNGLING

The Yngling (pronounced ING-ling) is the women's keelboat event, and their equivalent of the star. It had its Olympic debut in 200,4 and will appear in Beijing. The Yngling boat has a crew of two or three, and is designed to float even if it is full of water!

The Star is an open event. At the 1996 Games, it was won by Torben Grael and Marcelo Ferreira (BRA).

KNOW YOUR BOAT

Mast — holds the sails up
Tiller — controls the rudder
Rudder — used to steer the boat
Hull — main body of the boat
Keel — keeps the boat steady
Boom — holds the bottom of the mainsail so that it catches the wind
Bow — the front of a boat
Stern — the back of a boat

The fin on the bottom of a boat is called the "keel." It helps the boat sail in a straight line and stay upright. The keel on a dinghy can be raised or lowered by the crew, but the bigger boats in the star class have fixed keels that cannot be adjusted.

DID YOU KNOW?

The first ever Star class boat was built in 1911.

The Star event was first held at the Olympics in 1932.

Between 1948 and 1988, Durward Knowles (GBR/BAH) competed in a record eight Olympic Games.

PROFESSIONAL WEEKENDER

The instantly recognizable laser is one of the most popular single-handed dinghies in the world. It was originally introduced as a recreational boat called the "weekender," but it wasn't long before the laser became a favorite in competitive events. The boat made its Olympic debut in 1996.

DID YOU KNOW?

❓ Women have always been allowed to compete against men in the Olympics, but it was not until 1984 that they had their own sailing events.

❓ It is thought that sailing originated in the Netherlands. The word "yacht" is believed to have come from the Dutch word "jacht" which refers to a small, fast naval boat.

❓ International yacht racing began in 1851, when the New York Yacht Club raced their yacht, named America, around the Isle of Wight in Britain. This competition went on to become the modern day "America's Cup."

Laura Baldwin (GBR)

Robert Scheidt (BRA)

This is a new event, so no records exist.

SINGLE-HANDED DINGHIES

There will be three single-handed dinghy events at the Beijing Olympics: the Finn, the Laser and — making its debut at Beijing — the Laser Radial.

FINN-TASTIC!

The Finn is considered the finest single-handed craft by yachtspeople around the world. It is sailed in more countries than any other single-handed boat and has been in every Olympic Games since 1952. To sail a Finn, an athlete needs to be physically strong, adept at sailing techniques, and a clever strategist!

A FAST AND FELIXIBLE FIRST

The laser radial is a small, lightweight boat that will replace the Europe as the women's single-handed event at Beijing. The radial is a lot like the laser — it has a similar hull and uses the same equipment. However, the radial's sail is 19 percent smaller than the laser's, and it has a more flexible lower mast.

SUPER STATS

The USA and Norway have each won 16 gold medals in the sailing events — more than any other nation! Next is Great Britain with 14 medals, and then France with 12.

This is a new event so no records exist.

TORNADO

The event for catamarans at the Olympics is called the Tornado — so prepare to be blown away!

COOL CATS

Catamarans have two hulls, one on either side of the deck. They are much lighter than other similar sized boats, enabling them to sail across the water extremely quickly. With a good wind behind them, they can reach a top speed of around 31 MPH (49.9 km/h).

Gloves help to grip the slippery, wet ropes.

Both crew members wear life jackets — just in case they fall overboard!

ANIMAL OLYMPIANS

You wouldn't get far in a catamaran if you were being chased by a hungry tiger shark! These fearsome fish can swim faster than even the fastest catamarans. And if there was a gold medal for eating people they might win that too!

HARBOR VIEW

The sailing events at the Beijing Games will take place in Qingdao, in China's Shandong province. The competitors will get a good view of the red "Wind in May" monument.

Lightweight rubber shoes with ribbed soles stop the yachtsmen from slip ping.

Some yachtsmen wear wet suits to help them keep warm, but others don't bother!

Roman Hagara & Hans Peter Steinacher (AUT)

FATHER & DAUGHTER

The great Danish yachtsman Paul Elvström took part in the Olympics for the first time in 1948. His last Olympic race was in 1988, when he sailed in the Tornado event. His partner in the race was his daughter, Trine.

Qingdao, China

DID YOU KNOW?

The design of the catamaran is based on an ancient type of boat invented thousands of years ago in Asia.

The course used in the Tornado class is designed so that the race will last about 90 minutes.

Catamarans aren't the only kind of boat with more than one hull. There's also a three-hull boat called a "trimaran."

SILVER: USA / **BRONZE**: ARGENTINA

Only
six lanes are
used in each
race.

The water on the
course must not
be more than
11.5 feet
(3.5m) deep.

DID YOU KNOW?

🎗 Rowing events at the Olympic Games used to be held on flowing rivers.

🎗 After winning the men's individual sculls in 1956, Vyacheslav Ivanov (URS) threw his gold medal up into the air — it landed in Lake Wendouree, Australia, and was lost forever!

🎗 Even though rowing events are now held on still-water courses, the water and weather conditions still vary too much to allow official world or Olympic records.

HORST FISCH

The course
is divided into nine
lanes, separated by
colored buoys.

THE COURSE

Sculling races, like all the other rowing events, are 2,187.23 yards long and take place on a perfectly straight, man-made course, which is sheltered from the wind. Its banks are sloped and covered in gravel to help absorb waves, keeping the surface of the water flat and still.

SCULLING

In the sculling events each competitor has two oars, one in each hand.

Katrin Rutschow-Stomporowski won a gold medal in sculls at both the 1996 and 2004 Games.

WINNING QUALITIES

Rowing requires powerful arm, chest, leg, and stomach muscles. Maintaining a steady pace with the oars is crucial and requires precise timing, which is why top rowers, such as Katrin Rutschow–Stomporowski (GER), also need a superb sense of natural rhythm.

Rowers wear lightweight shorts and vests made out of stretchy materials.

In rowing, boats travel backwards.

The color of the buoys indicates the distance to the finish line.

NEW ZEALAND

MEN: Single sculls: Katrin Rutschow-Stomporowski (GER) / **Double sculls:** Georgina Evers-Swindell & Caroline Evers-Swindell (NZL) / **Lightweight double sculls:** Constanta Burcica & Angela Alupei (ROM) / **Quadruple sculls:** GERMANY

SWEEP OAR (COXED)

Make way for the mighty "Eights," the largest and fastest rowing boats at the Games.

The cox is the only person in the boat who can see where to go!

WHY 8 = 9!

The Eights are "sweep oar" rowing events. Unlike sculling races, each rower has only one oar, not two. Eights are so called because they are rowed by eight people — although there are actually nine people on board each boat! The extra crew member is the "coxswain" ("cox" for short).

SUPER STATS

The boats used in the Eights are about 56 feet (17.1m) long long — that's over twice the length of a single scull boat!

IN THE DRIVER'S SEAT

The cox's job is to keep the other members of the team rowing in a smooth, steady rhythm and to decide how fast they should row. Coxes are also responsible for steering the boat and making it go in a straight line.

GOLDEN BOY

At the Games in 1900 (before minimum weight limits were introduced) one team decided that their cox was too heavy, so they asked a young boy in the crowd to take his place! The team and their new cox won the final, and the boy (name unknown and thought to be less than 10 years old) was presented with a gold medal.

Lightweight Eights (GBR)

he German cox next to one of his teammates, Barcelona 1992

LIGHT WORK

Although a light cox is best, there are minimum weight limits: 121 pounds (54.9 kg) in the men's event and 110 pounds (49.9 kg) in the women's. If the cox weighs less than the limit, extra weight is added to the boat to make up the difference.

DID YOU KNOW?

The cox in Olympic races must be the same sex as the rest of the crew.

A crew can continue racing if one of the rowers falls out of the boat but not if the cox falls out!

The youngest cox whose age and name were known for certain was 12-year-old Noel Vandernotte (FRA), who won two gold medals in 1936.

OARSOME!

Drew Ginn & James Tomkins (AUS) celebrate their 2004 win at the Athens Games.

DID YOU KNOW?

Competitors in coxless boats steer using a rudder that's controlled by pedals.

Competitors in the lightweight event must weigh less than 160 pounds (72.6 kg).

In 1980 and 1992, two pairs of twins raced against each other in the final of the coxless pairs!

The competitors' shoes are attached to a plate on the bottom of the boat.

The seats inside the boat are mounted on rails to allow the rowers to slide forward and backward while they row and increase the power of each stroke.

SWEEP OAR (COXLESS)

There are four other Sweep-oar rowing races at the Olympics, but there is no room for a cox in these events.

UNDER STARTER'S ORDERS

At the start of each race the boats are held in position by a device called a "boot." When the crews are ready, an official shouts "Two minutes!" and reads out the names of all the competitors taking part. If the light controlled by the judges has turned white, the official shouts 'Attention!" then presses a button that gives off a loud beep. At the same time, the boot automatically releases the boats.

THE EVENTS

The coxless pairs is a race with one event for men and another for women, plus men-only events — the coxless four and the lightweight coxless four.

LEARN THE LINGO

Bow — name also given to the rower who sits at the front

Stroke — name given to the person who sits at the back of the boat

Shell — another name for a racing boat

The boats are usually made of wood.

Rowing boat

The outrigger supports the weight of the oar, helping the boat to go faster.

CANOE

Unlike a rowing boat, the paddle that powers a canoe must not be fixed to the boat in any way.

ANCIENT ORIGINS

Native Americans made canoes from hollowed-out tree trunks, which they knelt in to paddle. Modern canoes are based on this design, but are much more streamlined than the traditional-style canoe shown below.

The paddles are no fixed to the bo and are used o either side.

Canadian canoe with oars

Today's canoes still partly resemble hollow tree trunks in shape, but are made of fiberglass.

Canoeists kneel inside the canoe so there are no seats.

PADDLE POWER

The paddles used by canoeists have a handle to grip at one end and a flat blade for pushing through the water at the other. The paddles are also used to steer, as paddling hard on one side makes the canoe turn toward the other side.

SUPER STATS

For many years the former Soviet Union held the record for the canoe and kayak events, with 22 gold medals. But the longstanding record has been beaten by Germany, which now holds 30 gold medals. Hungary has notched 17 golds.

IT'S A MAN'S WORLD

Sprint races take place over 547 yards (500m) and 1094 yards (1000m), and there are events for one-man and two-man canoes. However, there are no canoeing events for women.

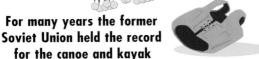

Martin Doktor (CZE),
Atlanta 1996

DOING THE DOUBLE

The sprint events are a simple headlong dash to the finish line. The winner is the first to cross the line — as long as the boat is the right way up! Both of the individual sprints at the 1996 Olympics were won by Martin Doktor (CZE).

DID YOU KNOW?

The different canoe events at the Olympics are often given letters and numbers. For example, "C1" means a one-man canoe race, and "C2" means a two-man event.

Canoeists are forbidden to ride on the wash (waves) created by another competitor's canoe in front of them.

Canoes are only allowed to have a tiny keel which mustn't stick out more than 1.18 inches (3 cm) from the hull.

KAYAK

**When is a canoe not a canoe?
When it's a kayak!**

TRADITIONAL DESIGN

Modern kayaks, like canoes, are based on a traditional type of boat. Kayaks were invented by the Inuit people who live in the Arctic. They would stretch seal skins over frames made out of whalebone then rub blubber (fat from seals and whales) all over the finished boats to make them watertight.

GOLDEN GIRLS

The women's sprint races are 500 meters long while there are 500m and 1000m races for men. As in the canoe events, there are races for both one- and two-person kayaks, known as "K1" and "K2" for short.

SPOT THE DIFFERENCE

Competitors in kayaks sit down to paddle, unlike Olympic canoeists who kneel. Another difference is that sprint kayaks have rudders. The paddles are different too — kayak paddles are longer and have a blade at each end.

Antonio Rossi (ITA)

SPLIT-SECOND VICTORY

After the 1000m sprint at the 1988 Games, the judges deliberated for more than 10 minutes before announcing that Greg Barton (USA) had crossed the finish line first — just 0.005 seconds ahead of Grant Davies (AUS)!

Greg Barton (USA)

By holding onto each other's paddles, several people join their kayaks together to form a raft. The largest raft ever formed in this way was made up of 648 different kayaks.

DID YOU KNOW?

⅄ Between 1948 and 1960, Gert Fredriksson (SWE) won six gold medals, a silver and a bronze in Olympic kayak events.

⅄ At the Games in 1936, there were separate events for "folding" kayaks, which could be dismantled and carried around in bags.

⅄ Kayaks were introduced to Europe 150 years ago by an English lawyer named John MacGregor.

Antonio Rossi (ITA) won the gold medal at the 1996 Games in the Men's K1 500m single and K2 1000m races.

WOMEN: **Kayak single 500**: Natasa Janics (HUN) / **Kayak double 500**: Katalin Kovács & Natasa Janics (HUN)
The women's kayak single and double 1000 events were not held at the last Games.

KAYAK: FOURS

When traveling at full speed, competitors in the four-person kayak can paddle at up to 130 strokes per minute — that's more than two strokes every second!

PULLING TOGETHER

This picture was taken during the women's fours event at the 1996 Olympics. Look closely, and you will see how every member of each team is holding her paddle in almost exactly the same position. In kayak and canoe events, as in rowing, precise rhythm and timing are the key to success.

SUPER STATS

A four-person kayak has a top speed of more than 7 MPH (11.3 km/h) — that's fast enough to pull someone along on water-skis!

Look carefully at the paddle. Notice how the blades at each end are set at different angles. This means that as one blade is being pulled flat-side-on through the water, the other is cutting through the air thin-side-on.

Women's kayak fours, Atlanta 1996

CLEAN SWEEP

At the 1996 Games in Atlanta, the men's and women's K4 events were both won by the teams from Germany. It was the first time that one nation had won both events at the same Games.

Flat water canoe

DID YOU KNOW?

The four-person kayak made its Olympic debut in 1964.

Women took part in the event for the first time in 1984.

The men's K4 race is twice as long as the women's event. Men race over 1000 yards (914m) while women compete over 500 yards (457m).

READY, SET, GO!

Kayak races are started by an official stationed in a small hut alongside the starting line. When all the competitors are ready, the starter shouts "Attention, please," then fires a starting pistol. A competitor who jumps the gun twice and makes two false starts is disqualified.

NO PENALTIES

Canoeists in the slalom events try to go around the course as quickly as possible, avoiding penalties. A two-second penalty is added on to the final time if they (or their paddles or canoes) touch one of the gate poles. Missing a gate incurs a massive 50-second penalty!

Green-and-white poles mark down-stream gates.

DID YOU KNOW?

In 1992, 12-time World Champion Jon Lugbill (USA) finished the course in the fastest time, but missed out on a medal because his life jacket just touched a pole on the second-last gate!

Competitors start the course at 180-second intervals.

Slalom events in canoes, like the sprint events, are a men-only competition.

Michal Martikan (SVK) was only 17 years old when he won the gold medal in the individual slalom event at the 1996 Games.

Michal Martikan, Men's C1 slalom, Atlanta 1996

SLALOM CANOES

The boats used in slalom events are wider and shorter than the ones used in sprint races, and the top of a slalom canoe is covered over to prevent water from coming in over the sides. Canoeists paddle while kneeling down using a paddle with only one blade.

CANOE: SLALOM

In the sprint events, the water is flat and still, but in the slalom events, canoeists must battle against a raging torrent!

Red-and-white poles mark up-stream gates.

SPLASHING OUT

Water rushes down the 328 yard (299.9m) slalom course creating swirling whirlpools and powerful currents. Along the course are 25 "gates" that competitors must pass though without touching. Six of the gates must be negotiated up-stream.

U DIG?

The U-shaped slalom course at the Beijing Olympics is completely man-made. Workers dug out millions of yards of earth to complete it!

SUPER STATS

The artificial slalom in Beijing can be easily adjusted to set the level of difficulty of the course.

KAYAK: SLALOM

Unlike sprint kayaks, the boats used in slalom events must not have rudders. Instead, the competitors must steer by paddling.

All competitors in the slalom events must wear safety helmets.

FINISH

Kayak slalom course

KEEPING A WATCHFUL EYE

Up to three judges watch each gate on the course to see if the competitors touch them as they go through. All decisions are based on what the judges see with the naked eye.

SUPER STATS

In 1987, a British canoeist performed 1,000 Eskimo rolls in just 34 minutes, setting a new world record!

ROLLOVER

The power of the water tumbling down the course is often enough to capsize the boats and turn them upside down. But competitors just stay inside their canoe and paddle underwater to turn the right way up again. This technique is known as an "Eskimo roll."

There are events for both men and women in the kayak slalom.

Life jackets are essential in all slalom events.

DID YOU KNOW?

❔ Before the 1972 Olympics, the East German team spent months practicing on an exact replica of the artificial river that had been built for the Games. They went on to win all of the Gold medals!

❔ The layout of the gates is redesigned for the final of each event.

❔ Competitors from over 30 different countries will take part in the slalom events at the 2004 Games.

Competitors in the slalom events wear a "spray deck" around their middles. This stretches across the top of the cockpit and makes it watertight.

The hole in which the competitor sits is called the "cockpit."

PUMP IT UP

Because Beijing's slalom course is not a natural flowing river, powerful pumps are needed to push the water at the bottom of the course back up to the top again.

Stepanka Hilgertova, Atlanta 1996

Women's kayak singles: Elena Kaliská (SVK)

INDEX

COUNTRY ABBREVIATIONS

AUS	–	Australia	NOR –	Norway
BAH	–	Bahamas	NZL –	New Zealand
BLR	–	Belarus	POL –	Poland
BRA	–	Brazil	ROM –	Romania
CAN	–	Canada	SUI –	Switzerland
CZE	–	Czech Republic (from 1994)	SVK –	Slovakia
DEN	–	Denmark	SWE –	Sweden
ESP	–	Spain	UKR –	Ukraine
FRA	–	France	URS –	Soviet Union (1922–1992)
GBR	–	Great Britain	USA –	United States of America
GER	–	Germany		
GRE	–	Greece		
HKG	–	Hong Kong, China		
HUN	–	Hungary		
ISR	–	Israel		
ITA	–	Italy		